The Daily Shift

The Daily Shift

Matthew Petchinsky

The Daily Shift: Simple Practices for Lasting Transformation
By: Matthew Petchinsky

Introduction

In the pursuit of extraordinary change, we often imagine monumental efforts and sweeping transformations. Yet, the reality of lasting change is rooted in simplicity. Extraordinary achievements are not born from rare bursts of inspiration but from consistent, intentional practices woven into our daily lives. It is in the small, seemingly inconsequential shifts that the seeds of transformation are sown, nurtured, and brought to fruition. This is the essence of daily practice: a commitment to incremental progress that ultimately redefines who we are and what we can achieve.

How Daily Practices Create Extraordinary Change

Consider the power of a single drop of water. By itself, it seems insignificant—barely capable of making a dent in the vastness of a rock or shaping the contours of a landscape. But over time, as drop after drop lands in the same spot, the rock begins to erode, the landscape begins to shift, and the environment is forever transformed. Daily practices work in much the same way. They may seem small in the moment, but their cumulative power is profound.

Daily habits create a foundation for growth. They anchor us amidst life's unpredictability and provide a structure for progress. More importantly, they align our intentions with our actions, ensuring that the goals we dream of become more than aspirations—they become achievable realities.

Whether it's writing a single page of a book, practicing mindfulness for ten minutes, or taking a short walk each morning, these practices compound over time. They build momentum, creating a ripple effect that extends beyond the specific habit itself. For example, starting each day with gratitude can rewire your brain to notice the positive aspects of life, cultivating optimism that touches every interaction, decision, and experience.

Why Transformation Starts with Small Shifts

The prospect of transformation often feels overwhelming. We look at the gap between where we are and where we want to be, and it seems insurmountable. But transformation doesn't demand immediate leaps or drastic overhauls—it begins with the smallest shifts in perspective, behavior, and intention.

These small shifts are critical because they are manageable, sustainable, and realistic. They bypass the paralysis of perfectionism and procrastination, enabling us to act. Small changes invite consistency, and consistency breeds trust in ourselves. Each small success reinforces the belief that we are capable of growth, creating a virtuous cycle of improvement and achievement.

Moreover, small shifts are deceptively powerful. When we change even one aspect of our daily routine, it sets off a cascade of interconnected changes. For example, deciding to drink more water each day can lead to improved physical health, increased energy, better focus, and even a greater sense of self-discipline. These changes, in turn, influence our productivity, relationships, and overall well-being, creating a domino effect that can transform our lives in ways we never anticipated.

Transformation also relies on the principle of kaizen, a Japanese philosophy of continuous improvement. Kaizen teaches that even the smallest steps forward are valuable. By breaking down daunting goals into bite-sized actions, we reduce resistance and cultivate a mindset of progress over perfection. Over time, these micro-adjustments coalesce into a lifestyle that supports our highest aspirations.

The Path Ahead

This book is a journey into the art of transformation through daily practices and small shifts. It is a guide for those who wish to reimagine their lives by embracing the power of consistent, incremental change. As you move through its pages, you will uncover strategies for cultivating habits, overcoming resistance, and harnessing the momentum of small actions to achieve extraordinary results.

By the end, you'll understand that the secret to transformation isn't found in extraordinary effort but in the commitment to show up daily for yourself and your goals. Remember: the greatest achievements often have the humblest beginnings. A single step forward, taken repeatedly, can lead to a life you once thought impossible. Let this be the moment you take that first step

Chapter 1: The Power of One Small Change

Change often feels daunting, as though it requires an immense act of willpower or a dramatic upheaval of one's life. However, the truth is that the most profound transformations begin with the smallest actions. A single, deliberate change—what we might call a micro-habit—has the power to reshape the trajectory of your life, creating ripple effects that touch every aspect of your being. In this chapter, we explore the science behind micro-habits, delve into the transformative nature of small changes, and share inspiring real-life stories of individuals who embraced this philosophy to achieve extraordinary results.

How Micro-Habits Lead to Macro-Results

Micro-habits are small, manageable actions that are easy to incorporate into daily life. Unlike major life changes that require significant effort and planning, micro-habits are designed to feel effortless, making it far more likely that they will stick. These small actions, repeated consistently, become the foundation for significant long-term changes.

The Science of Micro-Habits

The power of micro-habits lies in their ability to rewire the brain. When you engage in a small, repeated behavior, you strengthen the neural pathways associated with that action. Over time, these pathways become default behaviors—habits that require little conscious effort. This process is known as neuroplasticity, and it explains why small, consistent changes are more effective than sporadic bursts of effort.

For example, committing to flossing just one tooth each night might seem trivial, but it lowers the psychological barrier to starting. Once you've begun, you're likely to floss more teeth. Over time, this micro-habit grows into a full dental hygiene routine that benefits your health.

The Compounding Effect of Micro-Habits

The key to micro-habits is their cumulative effect. While each action might seem inconsequential on its own, the results compound over time, much like interest in a savings account. One percent improvement each day may feel negligible, but over the course of a year, that small daily improvement leads to a 37-fold increase in your progress.

Take physical fitness as an example. Starting with just five minutes of exercise daily may not lead to immediate visible changes, but over weeks and months, this small habit builds strength, improves stamina, and boosts mental clarity. Eventually, the micro-habit evolves into a broader fitness routine, creating macro-results in physical and mental health.

Stories of Real-Life Transformations

Sometimes, the best way to understand the power of one small change is through the stories of people who have lived it. These real-life examples illustrate how embracing micro-habits can lead to profound and lasting transformation.

Story 1: The 1% Rule in Athletic Training

James, an amateur cyclist, struggled with motivation and consistency in his training. Inspired by the concept of marginal gains—making tiny improvements in every area—he decided to focus on one small change at a time.

He began by committing to cleaning his bike after each ride, ensuring optimal performance. Then, he improved his diet by adding one healthy meal per day. Next, he adjusted his sleep routine to ensure better recovery. Over a year, these small adjustments culminated in a dramatic improvement in his performance. He not only completed a grueling 100-mile race but also achieved his personal best time, proving that small changes lead to extraordinary outcomes.

Story 2: A Journey to Financial Freedom

Sophia, a single mother of two, found herself drowning in debt and struggling to make ends meet. Overwhelmed by the idea of tackling her financial situation all at once, she decided to start with one small change: saving $1 a day.

As she got into the habit, Sophia began to look for other small ways to save money, such as brewing coffee at home and using coupons. She also set aside time each week to review her expenses, identifying areas where she could cut back. Within two years, her micro-habits had transformed her financial situation. She paid off her credit card debt, built an emergency fund, and even started investing for her children's future.

Story 3: Transforming Relationships One Gesture at a Time

David and Laura, a married couple, were drifting apart due to the stresses of work and parenting. They decided to make one small change: sharing a compliment with each other every day.

This simple act of gratitude and acknowledgment quickly created a ripple effect in their relationship. They began to communicate more openly, express appreciation more frequently, and spend more intentional time together. What started as a micro-habit of compliments became the foundation for a renewed sense of intimacy and connection.

Building Your First Micro-Habit

The first step to harnessing the power of one small change is to identify an area of your life where you'd like to see improvement. Ask yourself:

1. What is one small action I can take today that feels manageable?
2. How can I make this action so easy that it feels impossible to fail?

Start small—perhaps by drinking a glass of water each morning, writing down one sentence in a journal, or walking for five minutes a day. Once the habit feels automatic, you can build upon it, gradually expanding its scope and impact.

Tips for Success

- **Anchor Your Habit**: Pair your micro-habit with an existing routine, such as brushing your teeth or making coffee.
- **Track Your Progress**: Use a journal or an app to celebrate your streaks and stay motivated.
- **Focus on Consistency Over Perfection**: It's better to perform your habit imperfectly than to skip it altogether.

The Big Picture

One small change might not seem like much in the moment, but its potential is vast. When approached with intention and consistency, micro-habits become the building blocks of extraordinary transformation. Whether it's improving your health, finances, relationships, or personal growth, the journey begins with just one small step.

In the chapters ahead, you'll discover how to identify, cultivate, and expand these small changes to create the life you've always envisioned. Remember: transformation doesn't require giant leaps—it starts with the power of one small change.

Chapter 2: Morning Rituals for Success

The morning is the most powerful part of your day. It sets the tone for everything that follows, shaping your mindset, energy levels, and productivity. By intentionally designing a morning routine, you can create a foundation for success that aligns with your goals and aspirations. This chapter explores the importance of morning rituals, how to create a routine that energizes you, and specific practices to set a positive and focused tone for your day.

The Power of Morning Rituals

Mornings offer a unique window of opportunity—a time when your mind is clear, distractions are minimal, and your energy is fresh. Yet, many people start their day in a reactive state, hitting the snooze button, scrolling through notifications, or rushing to meet deadlines. This chaotic approach not only drains energy but also sets a negative tone for the day.

Morning rituals, on the other hand, put you in control. They allow you to start the day with intention, focus, and positivity. A well-designed routine can boost your mood, increase productivity, and improve overall well-being.

Designing a Morning Routine That Energizes You

The ideal morning routine isn't about perfection or following someone else's blueprint. It's about creating a personalized set of practices that align with your values, goals, and lifestyle. Here's how to design a routine that energizes and empowers you:

1. Start with Your Wake-Up Time

Consistency is key. Choose a wake-up time that allows you enough rest while giving you space to perform your morning rituals without rushing. If you're not a morning person, start small by waking up 15 minutes earlier and gradually adjusting your schedule.

2. Create a Calm Environment

Your environment greatly impacts your energy levels. Set up your space to feel calm and inviting. This might mean keeping your bedroom tidy, placing a glass of water on your bedside table, or having a designated spot for morning practices like meditation or journaling.

3. Prioritize Hydration

Your body is naturally dehydrated after a night's sleep. Begin your day with a glass of water to rehydrate and kickstart your metabolism. For added benefits, try warm water with lemon, which aids digestion and provides a gentle detox.

4. Include Movement

Physical activity, even in small doses, energizes the body and mind. Whether it's a full workout, a gentle yoga session, or a simple stretch, moving your body releases endorphins and prepares you for the challenges of the day.

5. Fuel Your Body

A nourishing breakfast fuels your body and mind for sustained energy. Opt for foods rich in protein, healthy fats, and complex carbohydrates, such as eggs, avocado, or oatmeal. If you're not hungry in the morning, consider a smoothie packed with nutrients.

6. Set Intentions

Take a moment to focus on what matters most. This can involve journaling your goals for the day, writing affirmations, or simply reflecting on what you're grateful for. Setting intentions aligns your actions with your priorities and creates a sense of purpose.

Practices to Set the Tone for Your Day

A successful morning routine is more than just a checklist—it's a collection of practices that prepare you for the mental, emotional, and physical demands of the day. Here are some powerful practices to incorporate:

1. Mindfulness or Meditation

Starting your day with mindfulness or meditation helps calm the mind and reduce stress. Even five minutes of focused breathing or guided meditation can create a sense of inner peace and clarity. Apps like Headspace or Insight Timer can provide structure for beginners.

2. Journaling

Writing down your thoughts is a powerful way to process emotions, gain clarity, and set intentions. Some popular journaling techniques include:

- **Morning Pages**: Write three stream-of-consciousness pages to clear mental clutter.
- **Gratitude Journaling**: List three things you're grateful for to cultivate a positive mindset.
- **Goal Journaling**: Outline your top priorities for the day or week.

3. Visualization

Spend a few moments visualizing your ideal day or long-term goals. Close your eyes and imagine yourself succeeding in your endeavors, feeling confident, and overcoming challenges. Visualization primes your brain to recognize opportunities and take action toward your goals.

4. Reading or Learning

Use your morning to feed your mind. Read a chapter of an inspiring book, listen to a motivational podcast, or explore a topic that aligns with your personal or professional growth. Even ten minutes a day can accumulate into significant knowledge over time.

5. Gratitude Practice

Gratitude shifts your focus from what you lack to what you have. Take a moment to reflect on the people, experiences, or opportunities you're thankful for. This simple practice boosts happiness and fosters a sense of abundance.

6. Affirmations

Affirmations are positive statements that help reprogram your subconscious mind. By repeating phrases like "I am confident and capable" or "Today is filled with opportunities," you build a mindset of self-belief and resilience.

Sample Morning Routine

Here's an example of a 30-minute morning routine designed to energize and set the tone for success:

1. **5 Minutes: Hydration and Stretching**
   Drink a glass of water and do gentle stretches to wake up your body.
2. **5 Minutes: Meditation**
   Practice mindfulness or deep breathing to center yourself.
3. **10 Minutes: Journaling and Gratitude**
   Write down your goals, affirmations, and three things you're grateful for.
4. **5 Minutes: Visualization**
   Visualize your day unfolding successfully, focusing on your top priorities.
5. **5 Minutes: Reading or Affirmations**
   Read an inspiring passage or repeat affirmations to boost your mindset.

This routine is flexible and can be adjusted to fit your lifestyle and priorities. The key is consistency—showing up for yourself each morning, even if only for a few minutes.

The Transformative Power of Morning Rituals

When you take control of your mornings, you take control of your life. A well-crafted morning routine isn't just about feeling good in the moment—it's about creating a foundation for long-term success. By starting each day with intention, energy, and focus, you equip yourself to navigate challenges, seize opportunities, and move closer to your goals.

Remember, transformation doesn't require perfection. Even if you can only commit to one small practice, the effort will ripple out into every corner of your life. Start today, and let your morning rituals become the catalyst for the extraordinary.

Chapter 3: Mindset Shifts for Everyday Growth

Growth is not just about what you do but how you think. Your mindset acts as the lens through which you view the world, influencing your actions, decisions, and ultimately, your outcomes. When you adopt a mindset geared toward growth, you turn obstacles into opportunities and setbacks into stepping stones. This chapter delves into the art of reframing challenges, cultivating resilience, and employing techniques to maintain a positive outlook in the face of life's uncertainties.

Reframing Challenges as Opportunities

At the heart of growth is the ability to see challenges not as roadblocks but as invitations to grow. This mindset doesn't diminish the difficulty of challenges; instead, it reshapes how you perceive and respond to them.

1. The Power of Perspective

Challenges often feel insurmountable because of the way we interpret them. A failure can seem like the end of the road or a chance to learn and improve. The difference lies in perspective. Reframing requires stepping back and asking empowering questions, such as:

- What can I learn from this?
- How can this situation make me stronger?
- What opportunity does this challenge present?

2. The Growth Mindset

Coined by psychologist Carol Dweck, the growth mindset is the belief that abilities and intelligence can be developed through effort, learning, and persistence. People with a growth mindset view challenges as opportunities to stretch their skills, while those with a fixed mindset see them as threats to their competence.

For example, a student with a growth mindset might see a poor test score as a signal to refine their study methods, whereas someone with a fixed mindset might interpret it as evidence of their inadequacy.

3. Turning Failures into Feedback

Failure is not the opposite of success—it's a crucial part of it. When you reframe failures as feedback, you extract valuable insights and adjust your approach. This perspective transforms failures into stepping stones, propelling you closer to your goals.

For instance, consider Thomas Edison's famous response to his many attempts to invent the light bulb: "I have not failed. I've just found 10,000 ways that won't work." Each failure brought him closer to success.

4. Practical Steps to Reframe Challenges

- **Label the Challenge**: Name the issue and acknowledge its difficulty without judgment.
- **Break It Down**: Deconstruct the challenge into smaller, manageable parts.
- **Identify the Lesson**: Ask yourself what the situation is teaching you.
- **Focus on Solutions**: Shift your energy toward finding ways to address the challenge.

Techniques for Maintaining a Positive Outlook

A positive outlook doesn't mean ignoring difficulties or pretending everything is perfect. Instead, it's about cultivating a mindset that allows you to navigate life's ups and downs with resilience and optimism. Here are actionable techniques to help you maintain positivity every day.

1. Practice Gratitude

Gratitude shifts your focus from what's lacking to what's abundant. By regularly acknowledging the good in your life, you train your brain to notice and appreciate positive experiences.

How to Practice Gratitude:

- Keep a gratitude journal and write down three things you're thankful for each day.
- Share your gratitude with others by expressing appreciation or sending thank-you notes.
- Reflect on challenges you've overcome and the growth they've inspired.

2. Embrace Affirmations

Affirmations are positive statements that reinforce self-belief and resilience. Repeating affirmations daily can help rewire your brain to focus on possibilities rather than limitations.

Examples of Affirmations:

- "I am capable of overcoming any challenge."
- "I am growing stronger and wiser every day."
- "I choose to see the good in every situation."

3. Cultivate Mindfulness

Mindfulness involves being fully present in the moment without judgment. This practice reduces stress, increases self-awareness, and helps you respond to situations with clarity rather than reactivity.

How to Practice Mindfulness:

- Take a few minutes each day to focus on your breath and observe your thoughts without judgment.
- Engage in mindful activities, such as eating slowly or walking in nature, paying attention to sensory details.
- Use mindfulness apps like Calm or Insight Timer to guide your practice.

4. Surround Yourself with Positivity

Your environment plays a significant role in shaping your mindset. Surround yourself with people, content, and experiences that uplift and inspire you.

Ways to Create a Positive Environment:

- Limit exposure to negative news or social media.
- Engage with inspiring books, podcasts, or videos.
- Spend time with supportive and optimistic individuals who encourage your growth.

5. Focus on What You Can Control

Worrying about things outside your control drains energy and creates unnecessary stress. Instead, direct your focus toward actions and attitudes within your influence.

Ask Yourself:

- What aspects of this situation can I influence?
- How can I adapt to what's beyond my control?

6. Develop a Solution-Oriented Mindset

When faced with a problem, train your brain to look for solutions rather than dwelling on the problem itself. This shift reduces anxiety and fosters a proactive approach.

Steps to Develop This Mindset:

- Define the problem clearly.
- Brainstorm possible solutions, no matter how small or unconventional.
- Take one actionable step toward resolving the issue.

Real-Life Applications of Mindset Shifts
Story 1: The Entrepreneur Who Saw Opportunity in Failure
Jessica, a small business owner, faced bankruptcy after a failed product launch. Instead of giving up, she reframed the failure as a learning experience. She analyzed customer feedback, refined her product, and relaunched with a clearer understanding of her market. Within a year, her business became profitable, and she credited her mindset shift for turning failure into success.

Story 2: The Athlete Who Overcame Setbacks
After a debilitating injury, Marcus, a professional runner, was told he might never compete again. Instead of focusing on what he lost, he saw the recovery process as an opportunity to strengthen other aspects of his training. Through perseverance and a positive outlook, Marcus not only returned to competition but achieved his personal best.

Building a Growth-Oriented Mindset
Developing a mindset geared toward everyday growth is a lifelong practice. Start by embracing small shifts in perspective and applying the techniques outlined in this chapter. Over time, you'll notice that challenges feel less intimidating, setbacks become stepping stones, and life feels richer and more rewarding.

Your mindset is your most powerful tool. With it, you can turn adversity into advantage, find joy in the journey, and unlock your full potential. Every day offers a new opportunity to grow—embrace it.

Chapter 4: Evening Rituals for Reflection

As the day comes to a close, the evening presents a powerful opportunity for reflection, relaxation, and preparation for the day ahead. Just as a well-structured morning routine sets the tone for success, an intentional evening routine helps you wind down, review your progress, and align yourself with your goals. This chapter explores the importance of evening rituals, how to wind down with intention, and techniques for reviewing your day to foster growth and improvement.

The Importance of Evening Rituals

Evening rituals provide a sense of closure to the day, helping you transition from the busyness of daily life to a state of rest and rejuvenation. They also create a natural pause to reflect on your actions, evaluate your progress, and adjust your course for the future. Without intentional rituals, it's easy to carry the stress and distractions of the day into your rest, disrupting sleep and diminishing your ability to start fresh in the morning.

Evening rituals are not just about unwinding; they are about cultivating awareness, gratitude, and a proactive mindset. By ending your day with purpose, you prime your mind for positivity and growth, ensuring that each day builds upon the last.

Winding Down with Intention

The way you wind down in the evening directly affects your sleep quality, mental state, and energy levels for the next day. Here are key steps to create an intentional wind-down routine:

1. Disconnect from Technology

Blue light from screens and the constant stimulation of notifications can disrupt your ability to relax and fall asleep. Aim to disconnect from technology at least 30 minutes before bed. Use this time for activities that promote calmness, such as reading, meditating, or engaging in a creative hobby.

2. Create a Calming Environment

Your environment plays a critical role in helping you relax. Dim the lights, light a candle or use essential oils like lavender to create a soothing atmosphere. Keep your bedroom clean and free of clutter to foster a sense of tranquility.

3. Practice Mindful Relaxation

Engage in activities that calm your mind and body. This might include deep breathing exercises, gentle stretches, or listening to calming music. These practices signal to your body that it's time to unwind and prepare for rest.

4. Establish a Consistent Bedtime

Consistency is key to regulating your body's internal clock. Choose a bedtime that allows for 7-9 hours of sleep and stick to it, even on weekends. This routine helps your body anticipate rest, improving sleep quality over time.

5. Journaling or Gratitude Practice

Writing down your thoughts, emotions, or moments of gratitude can help clear your mind and foster a positive perspective before bed. This practice reduces mental clutter and encourages a sense of closure for the day.

6. Engage in Light Reading or Reflection

Reading something inspirational or reflective can help shift your mind away from the day's stressors and toward a calmer state. Avoid heavy or emotionally charged material, as it may disrupt your ability to relax.

Reviewing Your Day for Improvement

Reflection is a cornerstone of personal growth. Taking time each evening to review your day allows you to assess your actions, celebrate your successes, and identify areas for improvement. This process fosters self-awareness and ensures that you're continuously learning and evolving.

1. Celebrate Your Wins

Start by acknowledging what went well during the day. This could be completing a task, maintaining a positive attitude, or overcoming a challenge. Celebrating your wins, no matter how small, reinforces your progress and builds confidence.

2. Identify Lessons Learned

Every day offers valuable lessons, even in the face of setbacks. Reflect on what didn't go as planned and consider what you can learn from the experience. This practice helps you approach challenges with curiosity rather than frustration.

3. Evaluate Your Habits

Review the habits and behaviors you engaged in throughout the day. Ask yourself:

- Which habits supported my goals?
- Are there any habits I need to adjust or eliminate?
- How can I make tomorrow more effective?

4. Set Intentions for Tomorrow

Use your reflection time to outline one or two priorities for the next day. Setting intentions before bed helps you wake up with clarity and purpose, reducing decision fatigue in the morning.

5. Use a Structured Reflection Framework

To make your evening review more effective, consider using a structured framework like the following:

- **Gratitude**: What am I thankful for today?
- **Successes**: What did I accomplish or do well?
- **Challenges**: What obstacles did I face, and how did I respond?
- **Lessons**: What did I learn from today's experiences?
- **Intentions**: What are my priorities for tomorrow?

Sample Evening Ritual

Here's an example of a 30-minute evening ritual to help you wind down and reflect effectively:

1. **5 Minutes: Disconnect and Relax**
   Turn off screens, dim the lights, and create a calming environment.
2. **5 Minutes: Gratitude Journaling**
   Write down three things you're grateful for and reflect on your successes.
3. **10 Minutes: Reflection**
   Use a structured framework to evaluate your day, identify lessons, and set intentions.
4. **5 Minutes: Mindful Relaxation**
   Practice deep breathing, light stretching, or meditation to calm your mind.
5. **5 Minutes: Light Reading**
   Read an inspirational book or something that encourages a positive mindset.

Real-Life Applications of Evening Rituals
Story 1: The Executive Who Found Clarity
Lisa, a busy executive, struggled with overwhelm and insomnia due to the demands of her job. She implemented an evening ritual that included journaling her thoughts and setting priorities for the next day. This practice not only helped her sleep better but also improved her productivity and focus at work.

Story 2: The Student Who Improved Performance
Jake, a college student, began reviewing his day each evening to track his study habits and identify areas for improvement. By consistently reflecting on his challenges and successes, he noticed patterns in his behavior and made adjustments that led to better grades and less stress.

Building the Habit of Evening Reflection
Starting an evening ritual doesn't require perfection. Begin with one or two simple practices and gradually build from there. The key is consistency—showing up for yourself each night to create a sense of closure and intention.

Over time, these rituals will not only improve your well-being but also foster a deeper connection with yourself and your goals. When you close each day with reflection and purpose, you set the stage for continuous growth and success.

End your day intentionally, and let the quiet moments of reflection become the foundation for a brighter tomorrow.

Chapter 5: The 30-Day Shift Plan

Lasting transformation doesn't happen overnight—it requires a structured approach, consistent effort, and the right tools. The 30-Day Shift Plan is a proven framework for creating meaningful, sustainable change in your life. By committing to small, intentional actions over 30 days, you can rewire your habits, reframe your mindset, and lay the foundation for long-term success. In this chapter, we'll explore how to implement lasting transformation, provide a step-by-step guide to the 30-Day Shift Plan, and share tools for staying accountable throughout the journey.

How to Implement Lasting Transformation

The key to lasting transformation is not dramatic overhauls but small, consistent changes that align with your goals and values. Here's how to approach the 30-day transformation process:

1. Set a Clear and Meaningful Goal

Transformation begins with clarity. Define what you want to achieve over the next 30 days. Your goal should be:

- **Specific**: Clearly outline what you want to accomplish.
- **Measurable**: Include a way to track your progress.
- **Achievable**: Set a goal that is challenging but realistic.
- **Relevant**: Ensure the goal aligns with your long-term values and aspirations.
- **Time-Bound**: Commit to achieving the goal within 30 days.

Example Goals:

- "Exercise for 20 minutes, 5 days a week."
- "Write 500 words daily for my book."
- "Practice mindfulness for 10 minutes every evening."

2. Break It Into Micro-Actions

Large goals can feel overwhelming. Break them down into small, actionable steps that you can integrate into your daily routine.

For example, if your goal is to improve physical fitness, your micro-actions might include:

- Drinking a glass of water before every meal.
- Stretching for 5 minutes each morning.
- Walking 10,000 steps daily.

3. Commit to Daily Consistency

Consistency is more important than intensity. A 30-day challenge works because it focuses on repeating small actions every day, which helps build habits. Even on tough days, commit to showing up, even if it's at a minimal level. Progress, not perfection, is the goal.

4. Track Your Progress

Tracking creates awareness and accountability. Use a journal, habit tracker app, or calendar to record your daily actions. Seeing your progress visually reinforces your commitment and provides motivation to keep going.

5. Reflect and Adjust

Periodically evaluate your progress. If you encounter challenges, adjust your approach rather than abandoning your goal. Reflection allows you to celebrate wins, learn from setbacks, and refine your strategy.

Tools for Staying Accountable

Accountability is essential for maintaining momentum and ensuring success. These tools and strategies will help you stay on track during your 30-day transformation:

1. Habit Trackers

Habit trackers are visual tools that help you monitor your consistency. They can be as simple as a calendar where you mark each successful day or as detailed as a digital app that tracks multiple habits.

Popular Habit Tracking Apps:

- Habitica (gamifies your habits)
- Streaks (simple and effective)
- Notion (customizable tracking templates)

2. Accountability Partners

Having someone to share your journey with can significantly boost your motivation. Choose a friend, family member, or mentor who will support and encourage you. Check in regularly to share updates, discuss challenges, and celebrate progress.

3. Journaling

A journal is a powerful tool for self-reflection and accountability. Dedicate a few minutes each day to write about your experiences, including:

- What actions you completed.
- How you felt during the process.
- Any obstacles you encountered and how you overcame them.

4. Progress Milestones

Break your 30-day plan into smaller milestones (e.g., weekly goals). Celebrating these mini-achievements keeps you motivated and reminds you of your progress.

Example Milestones for a 30-Day Fitness Goal:

- Week 1: Complete three workouts.
- Week 2: Increase workout duration by 5 minutes.
- Week 3: Try a new form of exercise.
- Week 4: Reflect on overall improvements.

5. Positive Reinforcement

Reward yourself for staying consistent. Choose rewards that are meaningful and reinforce your progress, such as:

- A relaxing self-care day.
- A small treat after completing a challenging week.
- Investing in a tool or resource that supports your goals.

6. Visualization

Visualizing your desired outcome helps keep you focused and motivated. Spend a few moments each day imagining yourself achieving your goal. Picture the benefits, emotions, and sense of accomplishment that come with success.

7. Community Support

Join a group or community aligned with your goal. Whether it's an online forum, social media group, or local meetup, connecting with like-minded individuals provides inspiration, accountability, and a sense of belonging.

The 30-Day Shift Plan: A Step-by-Step Guide

Follow this structured plan to create your 30-day transformation:

Step 1: Define Your Goal (Day 0)

Spend time identifying your goal, breaking it into micro-actions, and preparing for success. Gather any necessary tools or resources (e.g., a journal, workout gear, books).

Step 2: Take the First Step (Day 1)

Begin with your first micro-action. Keep it simple and achievable to build confidence and momentum.

Step 3: Track and Reflect (Days 2–7)

Record your daily actions and reflect on your progress at the end of each day. Identify what's working and what needs adjustment.

Step 4: Build Momentum (Weeks 2–3)

As you settle into your routine, gradually increase the challenge if it feels manageable. For example, if you started with 5 minutes of exercise, try increasing to 10 minutes.

Step 5: Overcome Challenges (Weeks 2–3)

Expect obstacles, such as time constraints or dips in motivation. Use tools like visualization, positive reinforcement, and accountability partners to stay committed.

Step 6: Evaluate and Celebrate (Week 4)

In the final week, reflect on your overall progress. Celebrate your achievements, no matter how small, and identify lessons learned.

Step 7: Plan for the Future (Day 30)

At the end of the challenge, decide how to maintain or expand upon your progress. Consider incorporating your new habits into your daily life or setting a new goal for the next 30 days.

Real-Life Examples of the 30-Day Shift
Story 1: Building a Writing Habit
Alex wanted to write a novel but struggled to find time. He committed to writing 500 words daily for 30 days. By focusing on this small, consistent action, he wrote over 15,000 words by the end of the month and gained the momentum to finish his first draft.

Story 2: Transforming Health Through Micro-Habits
Emma set a goal to improve her health by drinking more water, walking 5,000 steps daily, and meditating for 5 minutes each evening. Over 30 days, these small actions improved her energy levels, reduced stress, and inspired her to adopt additional healthy habits.

The Power of the 30-Day Shift
The 30-Day Shift Plan isn't just about achieving a single goal—it's about transforming how you approach growth and change. By committing to small, consistent actions, you prove to yourself that change is possible, one day at a time.

Every journey begins with a single step, and over the course of 30 days, those steps add up to meaningful progress. Embrace the process, stay accountable, and watch as the 30-Day Shift transforms your life in ways you never imagined.

Appendix A: The 30-Day Shift Journal Template

The 30-Day Shift Journal is designed to guide you through your transformation journey with clarity, consistency, and accountability. This template provides daily prompts and reflection exercises to help you track your progress, celebrate your wins, and overcome challenges. By documenting your journey, you create a tangible record of your growth and build momentum for continued success.

Introduction to the 30-Day Shift Journal Template

Each day of the 30-day journey includes structured sections to help you:

1. **Set daily intentions**: Define what you want to achieve that day.
2. **Track progress**: Record the actions you take toward your goal.
3. **Reflect on your experiences**: Identify lessons, challenges, and successes.
4. **Maintain motivation**: Focus on gratitude and positive affirmations.

Use this template as a guide. You can print the journal, use it digitally, or adapt it to suit your preferences.

30-Day Shift Journal Template
Day 1–30: Daily Journal Entry
Date:
Day of the Challenge: (e.g., Day 1, Day 2, etc.)
Morning Section

1. **Today's Intention:**
   What is the primary focus or goal for today?
   Example: "Write 500 words," "Meditate for 10 minutes," or "Walk 10,000 steps."
2. **Affirmation for the Day:**
   Write a positive statement to motivate yourself.
   Example: "I am capable of achieving my goals," or "I embrace today's challenges with confidence."
3. **Priority Action Steps:**
   List 1–3 specific actions you will take today to move closer to your goal.
   Example:
   ◦ Outline my writing project.
   ◦ Schedule 10 minutes for meditation.
   ◦ Prepare meals to stay on track with my diet.

Evening Section

1. **What Did I Achieve Today?**
   Reflect on the actions you completed and any progress made.
   Example: "I wrote 600 words today and felt energized after completing my goal."

2. **Biggest Win of the Day:**

Identify one success, no matter how small, that you're proud of.

Example: "I finally completed a task I'd been procrastinating on."

3. **Challenges or Obstacles Faced:**

What challenges arose, and how did you handle them? If unresolved, brainstorm potential solutions.

Example: "I felt distracted during my writing session, so I'll try turning off notifications tomorrow."

4. **Lessons Learned:**

What insights or lessons did you gain from today's experiences?

Example: "I realized I work better with a detailed plan, so I'll spend 5 minutes planning each morning."

5. **Gratitude Reflection:**

List 1–3 things you're grateful for today.

Example: "I'm grateful for my supportive friend, the sunny weather, and the energy to pursue my goals."

6. **Tomorrow's Intentions:**

Set one key goal or intention for tomorrow to maintain momentum.

Example: "Focus on editing yesterday's work and planning my next chapter."

Weekly Review (Days 7, 14, 21, 30)
Weekly Reflections:

1. **Overall Progress This Week:**

What progress have you made toward your 30-day goal? Be specific about what you've accomplished.

2. **Key Wins:**

List 2–3 major successes from this week.

Example: "I exercised 5 days in a row and hit my hydration goal every day."

3. **Challenges Faced:**
   What were the most significant challenges, and how did you address them?
4. **Adjustments for Next Week:**
   What changes or improvements will you make to stay on track?
   Example: "I'll dedicate the first 30 minutes of my morning to completing my most important task."
5. **Motivation Boost:**
   Write a motivational message to yourself for the upcoming week.
   Example: "You've already come so far—keep pushing! Every small step matters."

End-of-Challenge Reflection (Day 30)

At the conclusion of your 30-day shift, take time to reflect on your journey and celebrate your transformation.

1. **What Goal Did I Accomplish?**
2. **What Habits or Skills Did I Develop?**
3. **How Do I Feel About My Progress?**
4. **What Were My Biggest Wins?**
5. **What Challenges Did I Overcome?**
6. **What Lessons Will I Carry Forward?**
7. **How Will I Maintain This Momentum?**
8. **What's My Next Goal?**

Final Thoughts

This journal is more than a tool for tracking—it's a companion on your transformation journey. By using it consistently, you'll cultivate self-awareness, celebrate your achievements, and stay focused on your path to lasting change. Remember, the power of transformation lies in showing up daily, even when progress feels slow. Trust the process, and let this journal guide you to the extraordinary.

<u>Message from the Author</u>:

I hope you enjoyed this book, I love astrology and knew there was not a book such as this out on the shelf. I love metaphysical items as well. Please check out my other books:

-Life of Government Benefits

-My life of Hell

-My life with Hydrocephalus

-Red Sky

-World Domination:Woman's rule

-World Domination:Woman's Rule 2: The War

-Life and Banishment of Apophis: book 1

-The Kidney Friendly Diet

-The Ultimate Hemp Cookbook

-Creating a Dispensary(legally)

-Cleanliness throughout life: the importance of showering from childhood to adulthood.

-Strong Roots: The Risks of Overcoddling children

-Hemp Horoscopes: Cosmic Insights and Earthly Healing

- Celestial Hemp Navigating the Zodiac: Through the Green Cosmos

-Astrological Hemp: Aligning The Stars with Earth's Ancient Herb

-The Astrological Guide to Hemp: Stars, Signs, and Sacred Leaves

-Green Growth: Innovative Marketing Strategies for your Hemp Products and Dispensary

-Cosmic Cannabis

-Astrological Munchies

-Henry The Hemp

-Zodiacal Roots: The Astrological Soul Of Hemp

- **Green Constellations: Intersection of Hemp and Zodiac**

-Hemp in The Houses: An astrological Adventure Through The Cannabis Galaxy

-Galactic Ganja Guide

Heavenly Hemp

Zodiac Leaves

Doctor Who Astrology

Cannastrology

Stellar Satvias and Cosmic Indicas

Celestial Cannabis: A Zodiac Journey

AstroHerbology: The Sky and The Soil: Volume 1

AstroHerbology:Celestial Cannabis:Volume 2

Cosmic Cannabis Cultivation

The Starry Guide to Herbal Harmony: Volume 1

The Starry Guide to Herbal Harmony: Cannabis Universe: Volume 2

Yugioh Astrology: Astrological Guide to Deck, Duels and more

Nightmare Mansion: Echoes of The Abyss

Nightmare Mansion 2: Legacy of Shadows

Nightmare Mansion 3: Shadows of the Forgotten

Nightmare Mansion 4: Echoes of the Damned

The Life and Banishment of Apophis: Book 2

Nightmare Mansion: Halls of Despair

Healing with Herb: Cannabis and Hydrocephalus

Planetary Pot: Aligning with Astrological Herbs: Volume 1

Fast Track to Freedom: 30 Days to Financial Independence Using AI, Assets, and Agile Hustles

Cosmic Hemp Pathways

How to Become Financially Free in 30 Days: 10,000 Paths to Prosperity

Zodiacal Herbage: Astrological Insights: Volume 1

Nightmare Mansion: Whispers in the Walls

The Daleks Invade Atlantis

Henry the hemp and Hydrocephalus

10X The Kidney Friendly Diet

Cannabis Universe: Adult coloring book

Hemp Astrology: The Healing Power of the Stars

Zodiacal Herbage: Astrological Insights: Cannabis Universe: Volume 2

<u>Planetary Pot: Aligning with Astrological Herbs: Cannabis Universes: Volume 2</u>

Doctor Who Meets the Replicators and SG-1: The Ultimate Battle for Survival

Nightmare Mansion: Curse of the Blood Moon

<u>The Celestial Stoner: A Guide to the Zodiac</u>

Cosmic Pleasures: Sex Toy Astrology for Every Sign

Hydrocephalus Astrology: Navigating the Stars and Healing Waters

Lapis and the Mischievous Chocolate Bar

Celestial Positions: Sexual Astrology for Every Sign

Apophis's Shadow Work Journal: **:** A Journey of Self-Discovery and Healing

Kinky Cosmos: Sexual Kink Astrology for Every Sign

Digital Cosmos: The Astrological Digimon Compendium

Stellar Seeds: The Cosmic Guide to Growing with Astrology

Apophis's Daily Gratitude Journal

Cat Astrology: Feline Mysteries of the Cosmos

The Cosmic Kama Sutra: An Astrological Guide to Sexual Positions

Unleash Your Potential: A Guided Journal Powered by AI Insights

Whispers of the Enchanted Grove

Cosmic Pleasures: An Astrological Guide to Sexual Kinks

369, 12 Manifestation Journal

Whisper of the nocturne journal(blank journal for writing or drawing)

The Boogey Book

Locked In Reflection: A Chastity Journey Through Locktober

Generating Wealth Quickly:

How to Generate $100,000 in 24 Hours

Star Magic: Harness the Power of the Universe

The Flatulence Chronicles: A Fart Journal for Self-Discovery

The Doctor and The Death Moth

Seize the Day: A Personal Seizure Tracking Journal

The Ultimate Boogeyman Safari: A Journey into the Boogie World and Beyond

Whispers of Samhain: 1,000 Spells of Love, Luck, and Lunar Magic: Samhain Spell Book

Apophis's guides:

Witch's Spellbook Crafting Guide for Halloween

<u>Frost & Flame: The Enchanted Yule Grimoire of 1000 Winter Spells</u>

<u>The Ultimate Boogey Goo Guide & Spooky Activities for Halloween Fun</u>

Harmony of the Scales: A Libra's Spellcraft for Balance and Beauty

The Enchanted Advent: 36 Days of Christmas Wonders

Nightmare Mansion: The Labyrinth of Screams

Harvest of Enchantment: 1,000 Spells of Gratitude, Love, and Fortune for Thanksgiving

The Boogey Chronicles: A Journal of Nightly Encounters and Shadowy Secrets

The 12 Days of Financial Freedom: A Step-by-Step Christmas Countdown to Transform Your Finances

Sigil of the Eternal Spiral Blank Journal

A Christmas Feast: Timeless Recipes for Every Meal

Holiday Stress-Free Solutions: A Survival Guide to Thriving During the Festive Season

Yu-Gi-Oh! Holiday Gifting Mastery: The Ultimate Guide for Fans and Newcomers Alike

Holiday Harmony: A Hydrocephalus Survival Guide for the Festive Season

Celestial Craft: The Witch's Almanac for 2025 – A Cosmic Guide to Manifestations, Moons, and Mystical Events

Doctor Who: The Toymaker's Winter Wonderland

Tulsa King Unveiled: A Thrilling Guide to Stallone's Mafia Masterpiece

Pendulum Craft: A Complete Guide to Crafting and Using Personalized Divination Tools

Nightmare Mansion: Santa's Eternal Eve

Starlight Noel: A Cosmic Journey through Christmas Mysteries

The Dark Architect: Unlocking the Blueprint of Existence

Surviving the Embrace: The Ultimate Guide to Encounters with The Hugging Molly

The Enchanted Codex: Secrets of the Craft for Witches, Wiccans, and Pagans

Harvest of Gratitude: A Complete Thanksgiving Guide

Yuletide Essentials: A Complete Guide to an Authentic and Magical Christmas

Celestial Smokes: A Cosmic Guide to Cigars and Astrology

Living in Balance: A Comprehensive Survival Guide to Thriving with Diabetes Insipidus

Cosmic Symbiosis: The Venom Zodiac Chronicles

The Cursed Paw of Ambition

Cosmic Symbiosis: The Astrological Venom Journal

Celestial Wonders Unfold: A Stargazer's Guide to the Cosmos (2024-2029)

The Ultimate Black Friday Prepper's Guide: Mastering Shopping Strategies and Savings

Cosmic Sales: The Astrological Guide to Black Friday Shopping

Legends of the Corn Mother and Other Harvest Myths

Whispers of the Harvest: The Corn Mother's Journal

The Evergreen Spellbook

The Mind Reset: Unlocking Your Inner Peace in a Chaotic World
Confidence Code: Building Unshakable Self-Belief
Baby the Vampire Terrier
Baby the Vampire Terrier's Christmas Adventure
Celestial Streams: The Content Creator's Astrology Manual
The Wealth Whisperer: Unlocking Abundance with Everyday Actions
The Energy Equation: Maximize Your Output Without Burning Out
The Happiness Algorithm: Science-Backed Steps to Joyful Living
Stress-Free Success: Achieving Goals Without Anxiety
Mindful Wealth: The New Blueprint for Financial Freedom
The Festive Flavors of New Year: A Culinary Celebration
The Master's Gambit: Keys of Eternal Power
Shadowed Secrets: Groundhog Day Mysteries
Beneath the Burrow: Lessons from the Groundhog
Spring's Whispers: The Groundhog's Prediction
The Limitless Mindset: Unlock Your Untapped Potential
The Focus Funnel: How to Cut Through Chaos and Get Results
Bold Moves: Building Courage to Live on Your Terms

If you want solar for your home go here: https://www.harborso-lar.live/apophisenterprises/

Get Some Tarot cards: https://www.makeplayingcards.com/sell/apophis-occult-shop

<u>**Get some shirts: https://www.bonfire.com/store/apophis-shirt-emporium/**</u>

Instagrams:
@apophis_enterprises,
@apophisbookemporium,
@apophisscardshop
Twitter: @apophisenterpr1
Tiktok:@apophisenterprise
Youtube: @sg1fan23477, @FiresideRetreatKingdom
Hive: @sg1fan23477
CheeLee: @SG1fan23477
Podcast: **Apophis Chat Zone:** https://open.spotify.com/show/5zXbrCLEV2xzCp8ybrfHsk?si=fb4d4fdbdce44dec

Newsletter: https://apophiss-newsletter-27c897.beehiiv.com/

If you want to support me or see posts of other projects that I have come over to: **<u>buymeacoffee.com/mpetchinskg</u>**
I post there daily several times a day

Get your Dinowicca or Christmas themed digital products, especially Santa Raptor songs and other musics. Here: **https://sg1fan23477.gumroad.com**

Apophis Yuletide Digital has not only digital Christmas items, but it will have all things with Dinowicca as well as other Digital products.